TIME

Etel Adnan

TIME

Translated from the French

by

SARAH RIGGS

NIGHTBOAT BOOKS
New York

Earlier version of these poems were first published in French by Tawbad:

"October 27, 2003" as *Le 27 octobre 2003* in 2008.
"Friday, March 25th at 4pm" as *Vendredi 25 Mars à 16 heures* in 2007.
"At 2 p.m. in the Afternoon" as *A deux heures de l'après midi* in 2010.
"Return from London" as *Retour de Londres* in 2010.
"No Sky" as *Ce Ciel qui n'est pas* in 2008.

ISBN: 978-1-64362-004-6

Design and typesetting by Kit Schluter
Text set in Italian Old Style MT and Hoefler Text

Frontispiece and Cover Art: Stele Sculpture by Simone Fattal (detail), with Arabic writings and drawings, varnished clay. Part of the "Garden Of Memory" installation at The Musée Yves Saint Laurent Marrakech, 2018. Photograph by Jamail Odredra.

Cataloging-in-publication data is available
From the Library of Congress

Nightboat Books
New York

www.nightboat.org

CONTENTS

OCTOBER 27, 2003

I say that I'm not afraid
of dying because I haven't
yet had the experience
of death

on the walls of an overheated
bedroom images on paper
fade like my bones in a bed

women love the night
which hides their
lack of love

they want clouds
casting no shadow over
the poverty of memory... while
their astonishment moves on

the autumn garden isn't enough
for our impatience. I am exiled
from my inner land since
a lost love left me

the hardened wood of a plumtree threatens
a galaxy unknown to all, and the
word borrows the reversible path
of light to bring relief

the tribes gather their bitterness on
market day; the sun fissures the only
fountain

Omar Khayyam asked me
to share his wine. I said yes. I shared
his melancholy and tomorrow
I will go see him in the earth that he
has become

with each being that is assassinated
in our country of sulfur and copper
a new will rises

voyage, oh voyage!
the final fire that ravages the air
unveils the soil on which
we walk aimlessly
and tirelessly

the hypocrisy of the strong protects us
from home. I prefer leaves
yellowed by the rain to false
victories

so I listen to the wind. It's good to live
where there's dying, where the legends
go out... our tombs will be as
light as angels' wings

let's not bother to fear those
who insult our insubordination
the conquered will always have the
last word

I live in an invisible that has neither
bathroom nor entryway.
the invisible has no owner.
the dream never has walls,
and it's never cold there

... and my shadows stretch
over my body as it sleeps,
and the sky stops being blue, and
the light waits

we don't have famous actresses
in our little grocery stores and our
men exported by hunger hurry
into the steel of winter

I am not a phantom along
the foreign river. neither leopard nor
owl. I am a current of air

if we write, it's that we can't
sing, if we sleep, it's that we
can't live

memory is good for nothing
most of the time: the hotels where I waited
have disappeared

it was forbidden for women
to go after love. so they
stopped looking for paradise

come on! jasmine behind the ear
belongs to a fallen dusk.
we'd like to stop talking about
human things, but stones
are no better

when she said that she was water
and light, they started to eat
something bitter and hard
in the dark ... that's to say they didn't
hear the storm

from the boat that took me away, I've
kept the nausea, and the scent of the oil.
from the city where I landed, I
remember a defeat and an
expensive restaurant

I too have crossed the plains
that spread to infinity, while
happiness is encountered only in
bedrooms

in order to perform, words dress in
Phoenician purple, and it's in the
spaces separating them that
great adventures take place

I plunge my hands into the sun
whereas sleeping bodies prefer
slivers of the moon

let's stay in the Mediterranean, not far
from the fields planted with orange trees
in bloom

those who cannot leave
discover the geography
of the body. there are also airfields
and harbors on the surface of our souls

don't leave the Mediterranean
without telling her that you loved her:
her daughters and her sons went
North, a day of rain, or a day
of war

as for me, I belong to the stones
thrown for lack of helicopters,
to the women locked up,
to the political prisoners;
sometimes I regret my love of
splendor

but our solar mother star,
and the lunar father, in their way,
have entrusted us with useless
objects from a forgotten century

in the water of certain rivers there
is a wild happiness

in Yosemite Valley,
with the color of the Pacific still
trailing in my eyes, I buried
the essential and the inessential. That
happiness will survive my death

my friend Khaled sends me palm tree
postcards because he knows that
Europe is covered in burned petrol

I pass by the trees of this
season as I pass by
men and women... I believe it's
possible to have loved only
shadows

I return to Greece, preferred friend of
celestial Arabia, because they have
horses in common, and wild teenagers

I close the shutters and I wonder
where the light went that married
the sea beneath our eyes

I'd have liked to go to the corner
café, to watch the cold file by while I'm
in the warm, or even to make love…
but bombs are raining down on Baghdad

this evening, my friends, I'm going to bed
early because the dark is too thick. I'll try,
contrary to what's usual in dreams, not to let
myself be carried by waves, nor hunt
for my key. I'm going to try to sleep,
I believe, as children do

there's a time in autumn when the
trees change their nature, and
wake up beyond
matter; then one sees them come back to
their ordinary selves

it's good to stay in discontinuity, there
where birds live, and to know that
nations feed themselves on plundering:
armed with this disappointment, we manage
to bear the unbearable

she used to drive her car on forbidden
ground and the suns hiding there
gave her a beauty itself
proscribed

I come back to Greece with the fierceness
of one condemned to death, knowing that it's
no longer a territory; I should build it up
again, but instead of getting tools I
dissipate in grief

don't leave the Mediterranean;
elsewhere, in all seasons, there are
nothing but snares, and the regrets
you will conceal will
strangle you

don't leave your childhood, and its
sorrows. the first desire will
accompany you to the last
breath. streets lead to
illuminations, but never to peace
of the heart

watch your brothers die
on TV, and don't move.
they are in a new world
although with no exit

Paris, 27 October 2003

FRIDAY, MARCH 25TH AT 4 PM

what is new
in my life: the discovery
of a mass of stars in the
Milky Way

to flee the hole in the air
created by a bomb in
a Baghdad suburb I reread
the words of Al-Sayyab

to ward off adversity,
time speeds up the appearance
of flowers   the children
play

trapped in our imagination
the angels appear in our
desires; the first light of day
makes them vanish

sadness punctures the walls of
the mind which then turns
into rice fields and trenches

walk on the perimeter
of your dreams. it's not
that the roads are blocked
but that the hearts have
given into the violence of the wind

absence. displacement.
waiting. then comes rejection.
anger follows. shame makes
the beds

the shadows jostle between
the walls of the scarcely visited cities.
time nips at our heels   we are
afraid to arrive last

I love the rain when it
wraps me like a
river. grafts me to the clouds.
I share in the properties
of the sky. I grow
like a tree

the souls of the dead   use
the television screen
tell me nothing
don't knock at my door

can spring age within
a few hours? the outcome
of this battle depends on
the answer to this question

a head riddled with bullets
filters the pain drop by
drop across the floor of the
kitchen where the family stands

when colored thoughts all
leave the hallways of the brain
the great paintings
where gazes are born
and die and go off

there are wounds
that wait for the heart
to dress them

she buried her face
against a mattress   the curve
of the back showed the loss
was unbearable

a bleeding, a windy
crossroads, a taxi. this is how
the days begin

everything falls in the autumn
of contradictions. the past
inhabits us in its most
poisonous forms because blood is
polluted with fat,
and thoughts

halos of cold gas
separate us from our origins. our
perceptions surf on a ray
of light
in the meantime I swim in the
afternoon sun toward
sensual pleasures... even though
they can only be spent
in the passivity of the body

the great apes were maimed
by men's jealousy. our
conversations remain faithful to
their banality

the sea is raging
and the earth rests on nothing

blue thunder bolts
argue over the solitude of every fragment of
Being, of every attempt to live

paradise lost doesn't amount to
a matter of palm trees.
and if I told you it was made
of sleeping bodies and early
wakings...

in the nonchalance of this day
the shadows are stretched out
under the trees to better
mingle with the night

we take the boat departing
for the islands   even as
the horizon travels to the rhythm of
our non-existence

drink a glass of wine, you'll be
warm inside, you
will think of Dionysus

we were born at the origin of
sadness   that's why our parties
are so dazzling. they end up
burning children and houses

stars go out
every few seconds; the time
it takes information to cross
worlds

I watched the sky a-sheep
with clouds; I saw Arab
poets sitting before a black coffee

I visited their efforts.
some sold their words
for a bite of bread,
others, their wives, but not one
of them relinquished his
dream

I would lay on sheets
bathed in my sweat. the month
of August in Beirut happens
without the world knowing

there is no other consolation
left to counter pain than
pain itself

desire intensifies on the
silver edge of the sea. my friends,
don't wait for me any longer, my heart
is in the abundance of the same
spring as yours

listen to the sound of your arteries:
they were formed in the image
of the great rivers of Africa
which carry more fire than water

the mountain becomes a razor
blade. the moon is eaten
by the eclipse. the women, in the
morning, swim to rid
their bodies of insomnia, sweat,
and unwanted kisses

me, I love still
sunsets.   I fear the day
as much as the night

AT 2 PM IN THE AFTERNOON

the sun came out at night
to go for a stroll and the divine crossed
the room. the windows
opened

writing comes from a dialogue
with time: it's made
of a mirror in which thought
is stripped and no longer knows
itself

in Palermo men are as
strictly trained as horses; or
else they have the shining violence of
flowers

it's more bearable to think of
death than of love

Greek thought explored
all things the way it
explored the islands

when men no longer have
power over women, over whom
will they have it?

all Sicily is painted
by the planting
of vines

the shards of grief that a teapot
transforms into inexpressible joy

the Barbary figs ripen
on brilliant mornings, with firm flesh,
with certain steps

limits everywhere; how to reconcile
soul and body, what to do between
two white sheets?

She said, standing in the middle of her ranch:
how black it is,
eternity!

on the other side of the street that separates him

from the garden's splendor, Issa sits
with a black coffee and talks about the mother whose
brain invents aberration

me I am sent back to the swamps
in the darkness of my doubts

the curtain falls on a mass grave. the Babylonian
gods now give birth only
to cadavers

philosophy is a non-knowledge:
thought takes pleasure in
measuring its borders

the body is a sacred place
because it bursts with life and lasts
briefly

time reminds me of those cemeteries

in which mountains are devoured,
enveloped in their mist

the cock crows   the dog barks
the cat climbs a tree

above the clouds and
before the moon ideas
drift...

and then the boats keep
returning to port, corn goddesses
protecting them

Shakespeare's will, written
on a piece of yellowed paper,
was handed to me one night
in London, when I was stricken
with hunger

over there there is nothing but rising
paths, a naked horse, clumps
of grass, wind

the permanent eclipse is expected.
it seems far in time, but
quite close in thought

the spider waited a long time but
the fly eventually came

and heat, what can we say to it?
talk to it about the cold, too late! about the
river? this one is dry. of love?
it is the most obvious
shape of it

the season passes a rapid hand
through the trees; don't believe
the wind is absent-minded,
that sleep is guaranteed

you say that the trains went too fast
but your madness raging over
       my body. was that nothing?

time can't be translated
your voice in my veins
grows its poisonous plants

roses are watered by
the black storms of our desire

the loved one won't go to the Night
Palace where women and wine
are waiting

so we don't speed up the illness
we pretended not
to love ourselves, knowing anyhow
the days would not come back

RETURN FROM LONDON

I perceive in passing
a crack in the
texture of the day

there are fewer and fewer
sailors, the sea waits
for the end of the living

soon I'm going to take
the train. then enter the
wall covered in red vines

it's not a question of
going down into the garden
time should
leave us

place gold crowns
on your heads
hell is not the sole
owner of fire

we call history the wells
brimming with orgasms. this tree is full of
its shadow

malediction is a curse,
a split, a look that
shuts—a blow to the head

some objects die
before us. pre-war,
the houses would collapse under
the furniture

freshness is missing this summer.
bread is missing also, surrounded by
prosperity. the space shuttle
has a hole in its stomach

thought derailed from the first
instant. I told you: go to
the mountain top, where there's nothing
left to be seen

fever took hold of time.
light is astonished by its own
brightness. thus begins the final question:
what have I done with my childhood?

attention has its origin in
an impalpable fog.
rainy days, we become
plants

don't lose this need to exist
which precedes birth. History
is born in immaterial places, and
follows fate

love is the subversion of
death. our survival depends on
the capacity of the real to escape
the assault of language

laziness—with its inebriating effects—
is the wine of the poor, and of those
who wander among them

there are loves that grow
like cancers. we attach ourselves
to them like the body to its illness,
the moon to the earth

we preferred absence,
pain and silence to the frantic need
to see you. we are going to pay for it
for the rest of eternity

I would like to reflect like a
buoy, thrown out from the depths
to the luminous mortal surface
of the sea

know that Greece is itself
a theater. it's there that thought
got up on stage and
blinded us with its transparency

that's where we went
without the powers knowing, in a lost
youth, with illegible landmarks and
empty hands

then the storm came. the wet boats
on the drenching sea exchanged
expertises. while we
hung onto the precariousness of our rooms,
to the moldy words of the father

and then, after a multitude of hours, of
fatigue, of departures, we pretended
we were living

and the young wait on some
beaches for the sun to repeat itself.
they want to leave, to die
elsewhere, like forest animals

family is the mother. she knows
she is the origin. she gave
the coming death; life, she kept.
she swells at a glance

don't break the young girls'
hearts. you'll take the train
of exile. bread will be hard under your teeth

me, I waited to grow up and suddenly
love burst in the middle of the street: I received
some of its mortal blows. that very person
disappeared

sexuality penetrates us with its
vertical descent. sometimes it holds off
its satisfaction until later,
hits the wrong target

there are beds in the hospitals
that keep their clients; dams
that disturb their waters.
demand accounts of your
destiny

one closes a book as
one closes one's life, on oneself

I knocked over the whitewashed
puppet on the table
and operated, transferring
my death to her

the pupil moved to the rhythm
of the heartbeat: it
is about Shostakovitch

people come back in our
dreams to bring us their truth
that which our eyes refused
to see, and for which they
burned us, in burning themselves

don't tell Khaled that the truth is
an error of reason for he will at once
go to the harbor and get   lost in the crowd of
travelers

light blinds the animals. they
await the night, she is more likely their
messiah than ours

I went out to see the sea from my terrace.
it looked at me. I understood that
I mustn't launch myself into
its fierce waves

put out your lights before going to sleep.
the sun kissed you, leaving
burns on your face. it
returned to its solitude

the cult of the dead is but an excuse
for leaving the poor to rot in
prisons. the cars wait

in a virtual clarity and space
visited by the divine, the birds sing to
candles' ears the pain of living,
for happiness is unbearable

NO SKY

I

There are no frogs
    in this vast sky
    no messages
there is no sky
    in this brain
    no words
no brain
    in this body
    no connection

the drought
    is in the mind
        and on the ground

They killed a man with
    a baseball bat
"Oh!" said the police
"what a poor game!"

No one knows all the beauty
    of California
    as much as I

she is a goddess stripped
of her mines

but she remembers
everything that we have forgotten

They kill the whales
    to make cat food
and cry over China
    for there are no more
    Indians,
        around here

I am half of the universe
will I ever be a whole being?
            silence
and empty garden,
more ephemeral than a cloud
I am a speck

II

In the proximity of love,
    dispersion,
    refraction,
time no longer measures itself
    against the body...
there is blood
    on certain roads
    and the perverse friendship of
    death

There is noise in our
hearts
an imperfect breathing
attached to ligaments:
    dull pain in the
    wrists
    and the folds

Describe the body
    if you can
and you will see how unlikely
your soul is

matter being our
    sole possession

Like the half-light where
the Pacific sleeps,
its solitude is made of gray
forms   it looks for its metaphors
in electronics, it only lives
in the pallor of signs

She, in the rose-colored song
of a bedroom, a deserted
love, and the lost time
of trees…

           at
the edge of the jungle
    don't enter the
    sacred element of the present

Time has burned
that's why in the
naked lightness of the clouds
we are held back by the
nocturnal voyage

III

There remain
the folds in the slacks
the curled eyelashes
and the vigor of the
muscles: he is
   dead

A clamp found
in a pasture,
… a horse stumbles

I am not
the touchstone
of the sky nor blood
circulating. At the bottom of the pages,
signatures sleep

Light in free fall
sounds like a stream
which is the language of
matter

Truths are
department stores:
you are going up,
you take the escalator,
you don't come back

In the tentative
darkness of the
raisins there was
half of the
            sun
then the shadow
of the past

Sometimes I get ready for the
    voyage of no return,
but dawn raises the curtains,
    and my adolescence
    is standing at the corner
        of nowhere

Under the wonder of
cold skies

some short circuits cross
brains
prisoner 116 thinks his
guard married Bessie Smith

And now, the sound
of autumn.
There's no more mystery
in my basement;
as for the garden,
it's as white as roses

These are solitary
islands:
their renown is based
on the death of Indians,
which imagination recovers

A bull whirling
in the sky and the
distance between you and
me lying in
a plate: what
is there to say?

between one war and
another, always
a gray area

She was locked in,
found a doorway
out: suicide.
her mirror heard the
shots

Paris:
    the deserts inhabited
    by Rimbaud,
    the nights of Ramadan
    visited by Nerval,
    Baudelaire, on
        the backstairs...

Night's arrival
in the middle of the dream
cuts life in
pieces.
    Power accelerates
        death

The mountain draws
   its clouds
light trembles
   above the chaparral
desire leaves this body

It's not a tree
standing at my door but
the knight of nothingness.
song is a sense that
joins our other senses

In the splendor of the
gray morning,
in the death camp
of Beit Sahour,
with a little dew
and a handful of clay,
   we created
                  life

IV

Around the ruptures
circles
appear

When the heart ceases to
mark the hour, grass
grows at the edge of
    scars

Love; a freshness of
    time,
the annihilation of the body by
    the body,
the liberation of
    the mind

And here is my landscape:
a neighbor turned over to the Authorities,
a messenger who's late,
joints resisting
the pressures of absence

There are arteries,
veins, and other channels
that all lead to death

But the conditions of ecstasy
are the same as those for terror
the loss of Spain
started the angels'
     rising
toward refusal.
Useless, this love

Over there, where everything is
     green,
plants grow so as to
     say nothing

Being is single,
like rivers,
it goes down; like gardens,
it goes out on the verge of
the absolute

V

Surprised by the persistence
of the waves the sea recedes
to the skyline

The heart sets up its equations
while history unfurls
in the bedroom

VI

Where to look?
Inside, the same
objects, the same
obstacles as there, before
you

the quantity
of ocean produced
by matter frightens us

VII

We break
no opacity while the
greatest dancer is still
suspended in madness

VIII

this morning I killed a fly
had I been a State
I would have destroyed a city

Separation acts like
Greek music   it
pierces the viscera, is no
consolation at all

The sun flat on my hand.
Sex, hidden, at the height
of grass

Your brilliant teeth bit

It's always four o'clock
in the afternoon, the hour when
upon leaving school I had
kissed a poster

Some flowers
wilt tombs while
orchards begin
to blossom

I saw a sky without a sky,
an abyss in an abyss,
a door,
to nothing

IX

Death hanging from the trees
rises higher than the eye
thoughts don't project
shadow on the walls

At the edge of Good and Evil
the photograph of someone
gone gives birth to
illusions

Sky wind and noise
is this poverty of
vocabulary or indigence
of the world?

Fate stirs,

you remain still,
having become a thing among
things

As for him, he stood up,
out of politeness, because he
was looking for
his life

X

How to return to isolation
when there is no more time
in this eternity?

The war was our peace,
the storm, our
     sky,
pleasure: pain and
            howling

Today, the sun,
tomorrow, the sea,
and often Homer reciting
the Iliad in a city
in Arabia

XI

Why does the sky rounding
the mountains make itself
so scarce, and why this
look?

Everything turns into
breath, even
stone columns

My childhood knew nothing of the
power of women, they
resembled sheets
of ice

Blood, in California, has
a dark color and
unknown reasons

If it's not light,
Being is metaphor
  I am this thing passing
  before me

XII

She died
the day of the lunar
eclipse,
as she lived

Infinity weighs on the
body
and the sea is of treacherous marble

And here are my finds:
the perimeter of Crete,
the wells of the Great South, the
closed eyes of a love

The day is not made of
light, but of
will

XIII

I am the sky of this
royal tomb,
as vast as its night

The self is an image of an
image, a postcard

Words are sitting among
us but look at other
landscapes. Where are we?

XIV

To think that I was naked under the
waves and overhead, the words
forming islands of blood
and tears...

In the green darkness of the
garden we discover the sullenness of
an amputated warrior, and his
impatience

And now a secret:
I suspended the universe,
opened it,
then I gathered myself up
into a handful of ashes

XV

Follow me, the angel said,
before slipping onto
my shoulders. Wisdom
came running from every direction

Time uses a scalpel
on its own body. Night
is no longer enough for the contemplation
of our misery. It's cold
in this blue water

The angel, this stranger, is
the illegitimate route of
pain

XVI

I know the landscape you're
afraid to live in, woman
whose hair has been blackened by death…
your mouth had teeth of
pearls and nothingness

In not letting you forget me
I forced sadness to
spatter the walls

The rain will make its way through
your bones,
there will be a ritual and some singing,
    then we'll wait our turn

They burned your
body, dispersed the memory
over the ocean, and refused to
wake me in the middle of the
    night

A Parisian café closes its
doors just when the day
rises up from the chairs

I suspect that time no longer exists.
The sky will follow

XVII

We have cried enough
to wash your
body
but that body was
gone

In the empty shroud
a more bitter emptiness

The door closes again and gold
follows me in with its impetuous
transgression

XVIII

In a parallel sleep
I came back to a body and
love, there where time
never dared show itself

And so I can say that
madness sings in the morning
in a setting of water and dream,
its red coat worshipping the
sun

XIX

Beings and their shadow have
left the garden   the chairs
look at each other, asking if
they should talk among themselves
or be quiet

There is: a split sky,
branches cutting the air
an octagonal pond

There's no more night and
day has not yet been created.
     the angels don't know
     that earth exists

XX

The end of love pitches us
into purgatories or hells
    there's no need to worry
    about paradise

The sky will never
stretch far enough to contain the shadow
of this unhappiness

XXI

You came to bid me goodbye
in a sleep from which I would have
loved never to wake

I managed to forget that you
were perishable now
the storm is happening in an
underground world   I had reached
the end of my life   I asked you
to believe it

We should

know that the great vases
meant for the afterlife must
stay empty.

BAALBECK

I

I am not going to sing.
A temple existed for real,
its stairs are solid

the gods, unwilling to
let go of it,
danced,
then decided to die...

leaving behind
them,
although barbaric,
a sun that we loved.

In the sealed obscurity of the brain
plants grow,
and fish swim,
while we think we're seeing
landscapes, and looking
at the sea.

we will not know if life is reversible,
but written in the pain
a joy that hurts

even more,
as in the heart's desertion
memory's fingerprint.

2

Around here rain is made neither
of water,
nor of angels.

If the plain is
the color of
blood
the sky is closed

the youth of
the single blade of grass
trying to split this wall
keeps vibrations of Orpheus,
he, mirror of my soul.

3

With bare hands
I knocked on mobile forces,
arrived at the
semblance of shadows,
all substance having fled

we live in
what looks like
waves
and wind

Just like the gods,
we've left a land
heavier
than bunches of grapes
in mid-summer

like one closes the
eyelids of the dead.

4

The sea
is far away,
an horizon of
fever
in a sleep
broken
by the dream
of its own splendor.

This is not where
I am.

The seasons
contemplate the light's confusion
in the arid zones of our
thoughts

riddled
with bullets.

the mind holds
its breath across
these expanses of
stones

like a child
who has lost his
mother.

me, I'm going to spend
the night stretched out on
the heat that they
have kept.

5

The stream running
underneath the temple
is Ariadne's thread
leading me to the
Minotaur
-before getting lost in the cotton
fields

in the airless
labyrinth
a living mass
cries,
day and night

the goddess has left him
I bring him olives and
wine
but the god
has aged

Other than me,
only the wind knows the way
that links Arabia to Greece,
and our thoughts to this place.

6

Here, the air
is dry

the living escape in
the form of impeccable horses
that run there,
between Lebanon and
anti-Lebanon

the world has a perfect
intelligence

we own all the columns
standing
wherever they are
being the only ones
to care

The Mediterranean spreads
from the other side of the mountain
it suffers from the boats that cross its body,
but has survived Carthage, Plato or Mutanabbi
like us

(are they each alone, or talking together, how will we
    know?)
What's Memory doing among these stones that keep
    coming back,
she, older than Creation, - and anxious to say it?
Orpheus is walking in the village square
while the wind
jostling
the setting suns to carry us
to places where
History and Nothingness mix their
great waters.

7

We're sitting under
pomegranate trees that came from
Persia to live in this harsh land
—when they were allowed to travel.

On the roads,
passengers
speak of the Aegean Sea
as if it were a person

for them, angels are superfluous
because it was a time...

better consign them to oblivion.

8

There's something funereal about orgies,
in the time it takes to say it,
the earth
has already traveled enormous distances.

Where is joy then?
Chained to me, an horizon,
too close,
blinding.

9

On a wall,
there was a sculpted lion

the first animal I
loved was
cold

the second
showed me
the incredible depth
of the flesh

the stone
was in
the East,

love,
somewhere else.

10

Watch out for the past,
poison to our fields,

for these columns
which are trees,

with no spring
or winter.

There, abroad,
there are oaks
centuries old
that heard Napoleon's steps
going back up
the Rhone Valley,
to fall, further
north, on enemy
soil

any defeat
is the end
of a life.

Objects are
the children
of their
own shadows

Climb through
infernal jungles
as monkeys do,

enter the labyrinth
that you are.

13

Theseus followed the thread
to kill the Minotaur
his wife had deceived him with,
but the string broke,
and his anger fell on his son.
Some
sometimes remember him,
but that
only makes him
twice as dead.

14

There's a temple in Baalbeck
dedicated to Bacchus,
and in Bolinas a Night Palace
that Joanne Kyger
protects with her poems

under our
footsteps a ghost
rises and instantly
disappears
because our countries
keep going up
in smoke.

15

Work is an incurable
architecture inflicted
on ourselves...

I would like to be inside
an insanity that works
like a sky above
my head,
possessed by a nameless acceleration.

16

I am hungry for the ruins
where I was running
in prehistory.

I will travel,
motionless.

When I climbed up
the pink granite
to the summit
I saw the beginning
of Asia -
timelessness joined us.

Nothing is closer
to the sacred than nothingness.

18

The days are enclosed in
a bottle of aspirin
I tell you, I'm dying
but the process is not that stunning...
the sun is lying
on the tide of the century,
there's eternity
in the calendar of Being,
and, in my eyes,
a faded rose.

19

I will not come back
to hear Ella Fitzgerald
glide over the columns. Neither will she.

Clouds pile up,
turn into human
forms

on riverbeds
the same inscription
always dissolves,
then reappears,
as the sky has
already told me.

21

When no one is waiting for us
any longer, there's
death,
so faithful.

22

Broken souls are not anonymous,
no more than the geometry
reserved for my naked feet.

23

There are moments when
the past ceases to be a form
of the present.
Rain and tears
Look alike.

24

Syria has always been the mother
of chaos. A land parallel to
all the others. In the epiphany
of a sun to come,
breathless.

25

The olive tree in Delphi,
next to the temple of Sikiyon,
remembers the oracle
saying that
somewhere in the plain linking
the Red Sea to the Dead Sea,
music will
displace the sky.

26

Ruins are relics.
The lineage being of little importance, we're related to
  them.

27

Talal Haydar is closer to the truth than I am, being of
    this place.
He used to pick up the moon
between the stones and take her to his bed...
These days, he bends to pick up a flower—
finds traces of blood.

TRANSLATOR'S NOTE

The postcard is a medium Etel Adnan loves, and often when translating this work I felt echoes of the circumstances in which it began. On October 27, 2003, Etel received a postcard at her home in Paris from her friend, Khaled Najar, the Tunisian poet and publisher of Tawbad Editions. Spontaneously she wrote the first of the poem sequences in this book, each poem a breath or two, thinking of Khaled. In this way the poems act like a correspondence, a poetry of the postcard, from one Arab writer to another.

The translator occupies the recto-verso position of not being able to be fully on both sides, having to choose one language while thinking deeply of the other language, and of a third address which is the person or people "out there." As a poet and translator of poetry in French, I found myself in the autumn of 2005 at a café in Paris reading *Le 27 Octobre 2003*, and wanting to translate it. So I asked Etel if she was going to write/translate it also in English. Etel responded very simply and enthusiastically as is her way, "I'd rather you did it."

At first it felt like pouring water from one pitcher to another, to translate these poems, so clear and lucid and succinctly chosen was each word. One short poem on each page, with Khaled's facing page translation in Arabic, gave me lots of room to ruminate on which words to choose. Part of the passion of translating a first draft as I scrawl it into the book in pencil is partly that I can be anywhere. It has the pleasure of the postcard—writing vicariously to Khaled, writing as if you are Etel, writing to you who are readers in English: so many sides, positions, and dimensions. I was on a rooftop in Morocco when I first translated the little volume of *No Sky*, and can remember the cloud formations of that day.

Also part of the magic is that I found the work seeping into my own as influence. I recall Cole Swensen saying how to translate means you feel the other under your own skin. And, I would add, under and into your own writing. I wrote *28 Telegrams* dedicated to Etel, and then the *60 Textos* to Omar Berrada, and so on, all poems of address, grounded in the moment and current contexts.

Etel continued to write these series, and I gathered them as so many ingredients to produce what is this current book, *Time*, the first time they are appearing all together. For each sequence I would consult with Etel, and she would change a few words here and there.

In the final stage Alisha Mascarenhas, Jérémy Robert, and Cole Swensen made extensive comments which I integrated, so deep thanks to them, as well as to the many publishers and poets along the way who published versions of these translations, including Pierre Joris and his *Nomadics Blog*, Jerrold Shiroma and *Seedings* of *Duration Press* online, Anne Waldman as guest editor at *The Brooklyn Rail*, Aditi Machado of *Asymptote* online, Ana Paula and Rachel Levitsky and the whole *Belladonna* collective, and

Khaled Najar in a Tawbad edition also with Ryoko Sekiguchi's Japanese translations of *Le 27 Octobre 2003*. My gratitude to Karla Kelsey and Omar Berrada for their insight on the translator's note. Special thanks to Simone Fattal, an extraordinary artist, and Etel's publisher with The Post-Apollo Press, for contributing work for the cover. Etel and I together named the book, and are grateful it finds a home in Nightboat, where it joins other work of hers.

ETEL ADNAN was born in Beirut, Lebanon in 1925. She studied philosophy at the Sorbonne, U.C. Berkeley, and at Harvard, and taught at Dominican College in San Rafael, California, from 1958–1972. In solidarity with the Algerian War of Independence (1954–1962), Adnan began to resist the political implications of writing in French and became a painter. Then, through her participation in the movement against the Vietnam War (1959–1975), she began to write poetry and became, in her words, "an American poet." In 1972, she returned to Beirut and worked as cultural editor for two daily newspapers—first for *Al Safa*, then for *L'Orient le Jour*. Her novel *Sitt Marie-Rose*, published in Paris in 1977, won the France-Pays Arabes award and has been translated into more than ten languages. In 1977, Adnan re-established herself in California, making Sausalito her home, with frequent stays in Paris. Adnan is the author of more than a dozen books in English, including *Journey to Mount Tamalpais* (1986), *The Arab Apocalypse* (1989), *In the Heart of the Heart of Another Country* (2005), and *Sea and Fog* (2012), winner of the Lambda Literary Award for Lesbian Poetry and the California Book Award for Poetry. Her most recent books are *Night* (2016) and *Surge* (2018). In 2014, she was awarded one of France's highest cultural honors: l'Ordre de Chevalier des Arts et Lettres. Many of her poems have been put to music by Tania Leon, Henry Treadgill, Gavin Bryars, Zad Moultaka, Annea Lockwood, and Bun Ching Lam. Her paintings have been widely exhibited, including Documenta 13, the 2014 Whitney Biennial, CCA Wattis Institute for Contemporary Arts, The New Museum, and Museum der Moderne Salzburg. Numerous museums have presented solo exhibitions of Adnan's work, including SFMoMA; Zentrum Paul Klee; Institute du Monde Arabe, Paris; Serpentine Galleries; and Mathaf: Arab Museum of Modern Art, Qatar.

SARAH RIGGS is the author of five books of poetry in English: *Waterwork* (2007), *Chain of Minuscule Decisions in the Form of a Feeling* (2007), *60 Textos* (2010), *Autobiography of Envelopes* (2012), and *Pomme & Granite* (2015). She has translated and co-translated six books of contemporary French poetry into English, including most recently Oscarine Bosquet's *Present Participle* and Etel Adnan's *Time*. Sarah Riggs lives in Brooklyn, NY.

NIGHTBOAT BOOKS

Nightboat Books, a nonprofit organization, seeks to develop audiences for writers whose work resists convention and transcends boundaries. We publish books rich with poignancy, intelligence, and risk. Please visit nightboat.org to learn about our titles and how you can support our future publications.

The following individuals have supported the publication of this book. We thank them for their generosity and commitment to the mission of Nightboat Books:

Kazim Ali
Anonymous
Jean C. Ballantyne
Photios Giovanis
Amanda Greenberger
Anne Marie Macari
Elizabeth Motika
Benjamin Taylor
Jerrie Whitfield & Richard Motika

Nightboat Books gratefully acknowledges support from the National Endowment for the Arts.

ART WORKS.

National
Endowment
for the Arts
arts.gov